Murray

by Andrew Murray

Lang**Syne**

PUBLISHING

WRITING *to* REMEMBER

Lang**Syne**

PUBLISHING

WRITING *to* REMEMBER

79 Main Street, Newtongrange,
Midlothian EH22 4NA
Tel: 0131 344 0414   Fax: 0845 075 6085
E-mail: info@lang-syne.co.uk
www.langsyneshop.co.uk

Design by Dorothy Meikle
Printed by Ricoh Print Scotland
© Lang Syne Publishers Ltd 2015

ISBN 978-1-85217-081-3

Murray

SEPT NAMES INCLUDE:

Dinsmore
Dunbar
Fleming
Moray
Neaves
Piper
Smail
Small
Spalding

Murray

MOTTO:
Quite Ready

CREST:
A Mermaid Holding a Mirror in Her
Right Hand and a Comb in Her Left

TERRITORY:
Perthshire

Chapter one:

The origins of the clan system

by Rennie McOwan

The original Scottish clans of the Highlands and the great families of the Lowlands and Borders were gatherings of families, relatives, allies and neighbours for mutual protection against rivals or invaders.

Scotland experienced invasion from the Vikings, the Romans and English armies from the south. The Norman invasion of what is now England also had an influence on land-holding in Scotland. Some of these invaders stayed on and in time became 'Scottish'.

The word clan derives from the Gaelic language term 'clann', meaning children, and it was first used many centuries ago as communities were formed around tribal lands in glens and mountain fastnesses.

The format of clans changed over the centuries, but at its best the chief and his family held the land on behalf of all, like trustees, and the ordinary clansmen and women believed they had a blood relationship with the founder of their clan.

There were two way duties and obligations. An inadequate chief could be deposed and replaced by someone of greater ability.

Clan people had an immense pride in race. Their relationship with the chief was like adult children to a father and they had a real dignity.

The concept of clanship is very old and a more feudal notion of authority gradually crept in.

Pictland, for instance, was divided into seven principalities ruled by feudal leaders who were the strongest and most charismatic leaders of their particular groups.

By the sixth century the 'British' kingdoms of Strathclyde, Lothian and Celtic Dalriada (Argyll) had emerged and Scotland, as one nation, began to take shape in the time of King Kenneth MacAlpin.

Some chiefs claimed descent from

ancient kings which may not have been accurate in every case.

By the twelfth and thirteenth centuries the clans and families were more strongly brought under the central control of Scottish monarchs.

Lands were awarded and administered more and more under royal favour, yet the power of the area clan chiefs was still very great.

The long wars to ensure Scotland's independence against the expansionist ideas of English monarchs extended the influence of some clans and reduced the lands of others.

Those who supported Scotland's greatest king, Robert the Bruce, were awarded the territories of the families who had opposed his claim to the Scottish throne.

In the Scottish Borders country – the notorious Debatable Lands – the great families built up a ferocious reputation for providing warlike men accustomed to raiding into England and occasionally fighting one another.

Chiefs had the power to dispense justice and to confiscate lands and clan warfare produced a society where martial virtues – courage, hardiness, tenacity – were greatly admired.

Gradually the relationship between the clans and the Crown became strained as Scottish monarchs became more orientated to life in the Lowlands and, on occasion, towards England.

The Highland clans spoke a different language, Gaelic, whereas the language of Lowland Scotland and the court was Scots and in more modern times, English.

Highlanders dressed differently, had different customs, and their wild mountain land sometimes seemed almost foreign to people living in the Lowlands.

It must be emphasised that Gaelic culture was very rich and story-telling, poetry, piping, the clarsach (harp) and other music all flourished and were greatly respected.

Highland culture was different from other parts of Scotland but it was not inferior or less sophisticated.

Central Government, whether in London or Edinburgh, sometimes saw the Gaelic clans as

*"The spirit of the clan means much
to thousands of people"*

a challenge to their authority and some sent expeditions into the Highlands and west to crush the power of the Lords of the Isles.

Nevertheless, when the eighteenth century Jacobite Risings came along the cause of the Stuarts was mainly supported by Highland clans.

The word Jacobite comes from the Latin for James – Jacobus. The Jacobites wanted to restore the exiled Stuarts to the throne of Britain.

The monarchies of Scotland and England became one in 1603 when King James VI of Scotland (1st of England) gained the English throne after Queen Elizabeth died.

The Union of Parliaments of Scotland and England, the Treaty of Union, took place in 1707.

Some Highland clans, of course, and Lowland families opposed the Jacobites and supported the incoming Hanoverians.

After the Jacobite cause finally went down at Culloden in 1746 a kind of ethnic cleansing took place. The power of the chiefs was curtailed. Tartan and the pipes were banned in law.

Many emigrated, some because they

wanted to, some because they were evicted by force. In addition, many Highlanders left for the cities of the south to seek work.

Many of the clan lands became home to sheep and deer shooting estates.

But the warlike traditions of the clans and the great Lowland and Border families lived on, with their descendants fighting bravely for freedom in two world wars.

Remember the men from whence you came, says the Gaelic proverb, and to that could be added the role of many heroic women.

The spirit of the clan, of having roots, whether Highland or Lowland, means much to thousands of people.

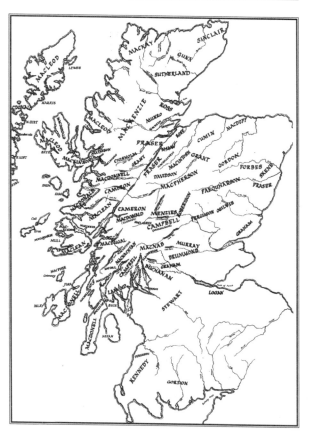

A map of the clans' homelands

Chapter two:

Family fortunes

The Murrays are the most titled family in Scotland and this is as it should be since their gift for leadership has distinguished them from the beginning of their history.

The family name is derived from the province and later county of Moray, one of the oldest political units in Scotland. The word probably comes from the Roman Murravia which meant a land or settlement by the sea.

In the early Middle Ages, as Shakespeare and Macbeth testify, Moray was as important as any part of the country. In fact it was only brought under full Scottish control in the 12th century when David the First destroyed the old house of Murray by forbidding its heirs to marry and gave feudal possession of the district to a Flemish knight. This military adventurer was probably the originator of the Murray family since he was soon referred to as Friskin the Murravia and founded a cadet line which acquired the lairdship of Bothwell and Clydesdale and was known in the 13th century as De Moray.

Andrew De Moray played a prominent part in the Wars of Independence against England and was officially superior to William Wallace in the Scots army that defeated the English at Stirling Bridge in 1297 and some historians think that he, rather than Wallace, was responsible for the victory.

Whatever the case, Sir Andrew was killed towards the end of the fight and Wallace acquired undisputed leadership of the Scots cause through the dark days which followed the defeat at Falkirk one year later.

The last De Moray, Laird of Bothwell, died of the plague in 1360, leaving only their magnificent castle, now ruinous, a testament to the family's power and, since the direct line had by this time died out, the chieftainship of the family fell into dispute.

Eventually in 1542 the line of the Murray Lairds of Tullibardine in Strathearn was

Some historians think Andrew De Moray rather than Wallace should be credited with the Stirling Bridge victory

recognised by the Lyon Court as chiefs of the arms of Murray. The descent of this branch is uncertain though family tradition traces it to one John De Murravia who was Sheriff of Perth in 1219. Certainly the first Laird of Tullibardine acquired his title by marrying the daughter of the Earl of Strathearn in 1284 and choosing to live with her in the Highland part of the Strath to the west of Crieff.

His son Andrew dealt a severe blow to the family's fortune by backing the Balliol claimant who tried to regain the throne on the death of Robert the Bruce. Though the rebels defeated a royal army in 1532, Andrew Murray was captured on a visit to Perth the next year and beheaded at Stirling Castle for treason.

After this abberation, the Tullibardine Murrays understandably kept quiet for several generations and the next Laird we hear of is Sir David who in 1430 married the daughter of Sir John Colquhoun of Luss who gave him no fewer than 17 sons and five daughters. We are told that all the boys slept in a monstrous circular bed with a single pole running down through the middle at which they placed their feet and hung their swords. On one occasion Sir David invited to his home King James the Second who was rather timid and lived in fear of armed plots. Sir David made the mistake of parading all his boys in full armour to honour the King's arrival. Next day James issued a proclamation making it an offence to parade private armies in the King's presence and had Sir David hauled before him for breaking this retrospective law. When the proud parent told him that all 17 were his own sons, the king was astounded and dismissed him without punishment.

Chapter three:

Conspiracy and murder

In 1542, as we have seen, the Tullibardines were recognised as chiefs of Murray. Their leadership was consolidated at the time of the Reformation in 1560 when the chief was one of the Protestant lords of the congregation who overthrew the French Catholic Mary of Guise and allowed the reformers to form their own government and establish the Free Kirk of Scotland.

In 1567 the Laird of Tullibardine and his younger brothers fought with the Protestant army against Mary, Queen of Scots and Bothwell at Carberry Hill. Before the battle, Bothwell issued a challenge to his opponents by throwing down his gauntlet and offering to fight whoever picked it up. Though the Laird of Tullibardine and his younger brother sprang forward, they were spurned by Bothwell as inferior in rank.

In 1586 the supremacy of the Tullibardines

was confirmed when the Laird succeeded in getting Murrays from all over Scotland to swear allegiance to him at a mass gathering at Perth. Among those who took the oath were Murrays from Perthshire, Stirlingshire, Dumfries and the Borders.

The power of the Tullibardine Murrays was further enhanced by two important events at the beginning of the 17th century. They acquired by marriage the immense estates and clan following of the Stewart Earls of Atholl whose line ceased in 1625. At one stroke the Murrays became masters of 200,000 acres covering most of Perthshire, more than 1000 of the most warlike clansmen and the strongest and most strategically placed fortress in the north, Blair Castle just outside Blair Atholl.

With all this, the Murrays rose quickly into the class of super chiefs like the Campbell Earl of Argyle and the Gordon Marquis of Huntly with immense land holdings and family connections all over Scotland and the unwavering allegiance of the broken clans who inhabited their estates.

The Murrays of Atholl won royal favour as a result of their service to King James the Sixth at the time of the mysterious Gowrie Conspiracy. The King and some members of his Court, including the Master of Tullibardine and his kinsman Sir David Murray, were invited to visit John Ruthven, the Earl of Gowrie, at his house outside Perth in the summer of 1600. During dinner the King was called out of the room by Gowrie and threatened with assassination. The courtiers, meanwhile, were told that the King had ridden off to Stirling and they all rushed off downstairs to their horses to follow suit. Luckily, James escaped from his guards for a moment and managed to climb up to a window, shouting "Help! Treason and murder!" to the knights mounting up below. The courtiers ran back into the building and, as Gowrie was hacked to death in the room where James had been held, Tullibardine and Sir David Murray chased Gowrie's brother down the back stairs into the garden where he too was despatched. The King was grateful for his deliverance and this, together with the clumsy character of the plot, led many to suspect that James had arranged the whole thing to rid himself of the two Gowries who were the most powerful noblemen of the day.

Whatever the truth, the Murrays were showered with favours. Sir David's family received the Gowrie Palace at Scone and the title Viscount Stormont. Lord Tullibardine was given most of the Gowrie land west of Perth and later, of course, the disputed succession to the title and estates of Atholl. Therefore when the great quarrel broke out between the next Stuart monarch Charles the First and his Covenanting subjects led by the Earl of Argyll, the Murrays of Atholl were amongst the strongest supporters of the royal cause.

Chapter four:

Civil war

The outbreak of the Civil War saw the beginning of a lengthy feud between the Murrays and the Campbells.

The first clash came in 1640 when the Campbells treacherously imprisoned the Earl of Atholl after luring him into one of the houses under a flag of truce. The Murrays took their revenge by contributing many hundreds of Athollmen to the triumphant army of Montrose who routed and massacred the Campbell army at Inverlochy in January, 1645. But the Athollmen were absent from Montrose's force at Philiphaugh in September, 1645, which was the only defeat suffered by the great Marquis. Lord William Murray, the Earl of Atholl's military lieutenant, was, however, captured at this battle and beheaded in January, 1646, on the orders of Argyll. The Murrays retaliated by sending 700 men against the force of 2000 gathered by the Campbells at

Callander. The Athollmen came upon their foes so speedily that the Campbells fled like madmen.

After this, however, the Covenanting cause triumphed and though all of Scotland rose against Oliver Cromwell in the 1650s and the Earl of Atholl led many Murrays to fight the Protector, the clan's star was dimmed until the Restoration of their Stuart patrons in 1660.

Under Charles the Second, Atholl became a Marquis and acquired the Sheriffdoms of Fife and Perth and even the Lord Lieutenantship of Argyll which was a great blow to Campbell pride.

In 1685 indeed the Marquis was given a warrant to exterminate the Campbells when Argyll landed in Knapdale to attempt the overthrow of James the Seventh. Atholl was instrumental in the suppression of the revolt and as Argyll was taken to Edinburgh for execution the Murrays laid waste Campbell lands, burning and wrecking what they could not loot and hanging more than 20 Campbell chieftains and clansmen.

By the time William of Orange succeeded the deposed James three years later, much had

changed. The King had alienated even the ultra-
loyal House of Atholl by his stubborness and,
when Dundee raised an army to attempt James'
restoration, the Marquis refused to join in, though
his second son, Lord James Murray led many
clansmen out in the Old Cause.

Meanwhile, Blair Castle was being held
for the ousted king by Patrick Stewart and was
besieged not very seriously by the Williamite
aide to the Atholl estate who doubtless took care
that his artillery scored few direct hits on his
future property.

The Marquis took a different way out of
the dilemma by going to Bath, to pump his head
full of political intrigue as one of his sons sarcas-
tically put it.

The battle of Killiecrankie was then
fought as Dundee moved to relieve the castle and
Major General MacKay brought the main Whig
army through the Pass to prevent him.

Dundee won the fight but was killed on
the field and with his death the Stuart cause went
into temporary eclipse.

Chapter five:

The blood is strong

For the next 60 years the Murray family was split down the middle by the various attempts to restore the exiled line.

The Murray heart was Jacobite but its head and purse were Whig. Though most of the clansmen and younger sons were active in the Stuart Cause, the Marquises and their heirs remained loyal. Their huge estate was too easy a target for Government confiscation to be put at risk. The loyalty of the main line was strengthened after 1703 when the chief was created Duke of Atholl and, though in 1715 his eldest son William and in 1719 his third son George were attained for rebellion, the Duke made sure that his second son James who became his heir was brought up in strict Protestant and Hanovarian principles.

On the eve of the '45 this son, Lord James, was in residence at Blair while his Jacobite brother and rival was entering his 30th year of poverty-stricken exile in France with the consolation that he was still referred to as Duke William by most of the clansmen at home.

The third brother, meanwhile, Lord George Murray, though still a Jacobite at heart, had obtained a pardon from George the Second and was living on the old Tullibardine lands at Strathearn.

Then came the news that Bonnie Prince Charlie had landed on the west coast with only seven followers, one of them the ageing and sick Duke William who was given the privilege of raising the Pretender's standard at Glenfinnan once the clans had gathered to support him.

Lord George Murray was now put in a terrible quandary. His eldest brother moved into Atholl and began recruiting for the Jacobite army. The Whig Duke and the London Government wrote to remind him of his pardon and his promise of loyalty to the House of Hanover. His wife was pregnant and strongly against what she called "this mad escapade!" But Lord George had promised himself that he would fight again for the

Stuart cause if there was a real hope of success. In early September, knowing that the scaffold or exile lay before him if the Rising failed, he rode off to join the Prince at Perth where, because of his military experience, he was quickly made general of the Jacobite army.

It is agreed on all hands that Lord George was the most impressive commander in the campaign which followed but he was not given full rein for his skills. He had to share direct control of the army with the popular but sickly Duke of Perth and both were subject to the overall control of the Prince whose inexperience was matched only by his arrogance. The Chevalier Johnson, a Jacobite officer who had extensive experience in Continental warfare, said later that had Prince Charles slept during the whole of the expedition and allowed Lord George Murray to fight for him, according to his own judgement, he would have found the Crown of Great Britain on his head when he awoke; and while this may be doubted given the massive superiority of the opposing forces, it is certain that Lord George's generalship in the victories of Prestonpans and Falkirk and even more in the marches from Perth to Derby and back to Inverness, often within sight and sound but never within the grasp of stronger Whig forces, was one of the great military exploits in Scottish history.

But his handicaps finally caught up with him at Culloden when the Prince insisted on giving battle to Cumberland on bad ground after an exhausting night march and while more than one third of the Highland army was absent foraging for food.

In the massacre which followed, the only redeeming feature was Lord George's charge at the head of the Atholl men on the Jacobite right wing. The Murrays pierced two lines of the government army before the clansmen were overwhelmed by a solid rank of bayonets in front of them. With raking fire from both sides and their own dead piled up below them, Lord George had his horse shot from under him after bursting through to the Whig rearguard and had to hack his way back on foot to his own lines in a vain attempt to bring up the Jacobite reserves.

Before this final defeat, Blair Castle had been besieged once again by its own family. First, the Whig Duke James had been driven from it by his exiled brother Duke William; then William in return, after entertaining Bonnie Prince Charlie in style, had been forced to retreat on the approach of Cumberland's army; finally Lord George Murray had led a force to recapture the castle in the weeks before Culloden. The siege lasted ten days and before beginning to shell and mine the fortress, Lord George rode to his Jacobite brother to ask for permission to destroy his property. As it was, the garrison was on the point of surrender when news came that Cumberland had left Aberdeen and that the Prince intended to give battle. Lord George retreated, firing two cannon shots into the west wing as he went, telling his brother at Inverness that he had never liked that side of the castle anyway.

The fate of the three brothers was very different. The Whig Duke returned to a much damaged Blair and decided to rebuild it in the

less fortified but still impressive style which it
bears today.

The Jacobite Duke William was captured a
few weeks after Culloden and was taken in a des-
perate state of health to the Tower of London where
he cheated the axeman by dying in July, 1746.

Lord George, after eight months in hiding,
escaped to Holland where he died in 1760, knowing that his son was likely to succeed to the
Dukedom and that, even if his cause had been
defeated forever, his own military reputation
stood as high as those other two great royalist
generals - Montrose and Dundee.

The Murrays of Atholl suffered little during the period of repression and economic disrup-
tion which followed the defeat of the '45. The
Duke was a Whig, his lands were comparatively
prosperous and Atholl was not amongst the dis-
tricts laid waste by Cumberland's army. But the
troubles which arose when the government tried to
enlist clansmen in the regular army show that it
was some time before London could be sure of
Highland loyalty. The Duke founded the Atholl

Highlanders in 1778 as part of the government plan to use recruitment to ease economic tensions and ensure that the clansmens' martial spirit was used in an acceptable way. The Atholl men were told, however, that their service would be for three years or the duration of the American War and, when both terms were up in 1783 and the government proposed shipping them to the East Indies, the entire regiment mutinied at its embarkation quarters in Portsmouth, assaulting many of their officers and holding the whole town hostage until the War Office agreed to their discharge.

An even more serious outbreak occurred 14 years later when the government tried to raise a Perthshire militia to deal with the threat of civil disturbance during the war with Revolutionary France. Ten thousand or more of the inhabitants of the Murray's estate rose up against the proposal, forming a series of rampaging mobs that terrorised the local gentry for several weeks. Finally one mob gathered menacingly outside Blair Castle. Atholl was forced to sign a humiliating pledge not to enforce the militia acts on his estates. After this, the disturbances died down and greater caution was shown in the enlistment of recruits and in the 19th and 20th centuries Atholl contributed many thousands of men to the armies which fought the great European and colonial wars.